His Feathers Were Chains

ALSO BY DENISE K. LAJIMODIERE

Poetry:

Dragonfly Dance
Bitter Tears
Thunderbird

Children's Books:

Josie's Dance (forthcoming)

Nonfiction:

Stringing Rosaries: The History, the Unforgivable, and the Healing of Northern Plains American Indian Boarding School Survivors

Stringing Rosaries won the following awards:

- 2020 Finalist, Stubbendieck Great Plains Distinguished Book Prize
- 2020 Independent Publisher Book Awards (IPPY), Bronze Medal for Multicultural Nonfiction Adult
- 2020 Independent Book Publishers Association—Ben Franklin Award, Silver Medal in the Multicultural category
- 2020 Independent Press Awards, Distinguished Favorite for Cultural and Social Issues
- 2019 Midwest Book Awards, Gold Medal for Regional History
- 2019 Midwest Book Awards, Silver Medal for Social Science/ Political Science/Culture
- 2019 Midwest Book Awards, Silver Medal for Cover Design

His Feathers Were Chains

By Denise K. Lajimodiere

North Dakota State University Press

Contemporary Voices of Indigenous Peoples Series Vol. 3

North Dakota State University Press
Dept. 2360, P.O. Box 6050, Fargo, ND 58108-6050
www.ndsupress.org

His Feathers Were Chains
Poetry by Denise K. Lajimodiere

First Edition
Contemporary Voices of Indigenous Peoples Series Vol. 3

ISBN: 978-1-946163-22-6
LCCN: 2020943287

Cover design and illustration by Andrew Stark
Interior design by Deb Tanner

Director: David Bertolini
Publisher: Suzzanne Kelley
Editorial Interns: Taylor Flakker, Kalley Miller, Corrine Redding
Graduate Assistants: Kalley Miller, Oliver Sime, Zachary Vietz

The publication of *His Feathers Were Chains* is made possible by the generous support of donors to the NDSU Press Fund and the NDSU Press Endowment Fund.

Printed in USA

Publisher's Cataloging-In-Publication Data
(Prepared by The Donohue Group, Inc.)

Names: Lajimodiere, Denise K., author.
Title: His feathers were chains / by Denise K. Lajimodiere.
Other Titles: Contemporary voices of indigenous peoples series ; v. 3.
Description: First edition. | Fargo, ND : North Dakota State University Press, [2020]
Identifiers: ISBN 9781946163226
Subjects: LCSH: Ojibwa Indians--North Dakota--Social life and customs--Poetry. | Indians of North America--Crimes against--Poetry. | United States--Race relations--Poetry. | American poetry.
Classification: LCC PS3612.A48 H57 2020 | DDC 811/.6--dc23

∞ This paper meets the requirements of ANSI/NISO Z39.48-1992 (Permanence of Paper).

In memory of Ginew

For Mom

Contents

Broken Glass Dreams

Identity

His Feathers Were Chains

Broken Glass Dreams

Pink Bedspread

Tearing up the old carpet, ripping off mop-boards
I bend to install new tiles and notice the pink
paint peeking out near the floor, a fraying slip
modest under layers of white skirting.
It was the Pepto-Bismol-pink that Mom had Dad
paint the bedroom, matching her hot pink floral bedspread.

Research shows the color can calm violent drunk offenders
in jails. It didn't stop him from slamming
her head against the kitchen cast iron sink, seventeen stitches
and a week in the IHS hospital. Coming out of the blackout
he denied hitting her and when he got out of jail
he was going to kill whoever did.

Drunk again and Mom yelling he was the one
so he should kill himself. He took all her sleeping pills
one by one in front of her asked if she was happy now
and laid down to die. His heart stopped three times
in the ambulance.

She died young at forty-eight, an accidental fall,
pneumonia set in and she gave up, weary of beatings,
arthritis, a stroke. He died this week, drink and three-
pack-a-day habit did him in. I finish the floor tiles,
replace the mop-boards, covering the pink. At home I lie
down, cover myself with her bedspread, a paler pink
now except for a corner, a violence, maroon.

Mare's Milk

Following buffalo and Red River
cart trails, the young couple

headed to Saskatchewan
by horse and wagon during

the month of ripening chokecherries.
Just across the border her pains

began and he ran frantic to find
a midwife. A baby boy, his first

breath sage and sweet grass carried
on hot prairie winds. She pressed

the infant's mouth to unyielding
breasts. Reaching their destination

the baby's kookum headed to the barn,
returned with a full bottle, having tied

up a colt. My father began life
with a belly full of sweet mare's milk.

Chain Smoker

He left his cigarettes burning
on the edges of dressers, tables,
kitchen counters, bathroom sinks,
leaving nicotine stains
and dark brown burn marks,
a dangerous brand.
My father was a chain smoker.
Memories like ashes falling,
Sunday mornings filled
with bacon grease smoke,
black coffee, farts, the roar
of baseball crowds
from the tinny black and white,
crinkling newspaper,
zing of flipped cigarette lighter,
crackling of lit tobacco,
sour overflowing ash trays.

My father was a chain smoker,
unfiltered Lucky Strikes.
He died of lung cancer,
his decaying lungs
suffocating. He quit once,
with the aid of anti-depressants,
the stench of regret.

Folger's Coffee

Dad's coffee was famous
throughout the reservation,
black as a spring-plowed
North Dakota field,
so strong it ate a jagged circle
inside his pink melamine cup.
He drank it black, cold or hot
fresh or a day old.
Could stand a knife in it.
Asked how he came to drink such strong
coffee he told of his aunt Veronica
making coffee on top the wood stove
in a large silver coffee boiler. She would
keep adding fresh grounds on top the old,
and boil again and again. One time his
grandmother came up from Ft. Yates
with a young adopted Sioux boy.
They offered cup after cup to him,
protocol dictated he couldn't refuse.

He got drunk on coffee!
Had to carry him to the wagon
and lay him down in the back.

Dad would get drunk at night,
lapse into a coma, yet get up
every day to go to work
as a carpenter, Mom making
him a fresh pot of coffee
every morning, filling his thermos full.

I asked his doctor how he could
do that—no apparent hangover.
He said that he likely kept a level
of alcohol and caffeine in his system,
that balanced each other out.

In the nursing home I tried to explain
to the staff how to make his Folgers
coffee. In this day and age of Mr. Coffee,
they were stumped, so I made coffee
for him in his battered tin pot
until he lapsed into his final coma.

Divorce

We drove to Bottineau
to hire a lawyer,
two hundred dollars in Mom's
purse gathered by crawling
into the bedroom, fumbling
through his pockets, stealing
worn dollar bills, praying he
wouldn't notice, his drunken
snores and change jangle my
nerves, Mom whispering
hurry. We never knew what
slight noise would rouse him,
the arm that held the army
rifle in the trenches swinging
swift and wide. We hid the money
in a cigar box at the bottom
of the closet but had to move
it the night he thought the closet
was the bathroom. The lawyer
shook his head at our money,
said he would need another
hundred at least. We drove home
in silence, my throat aching for Mom,
her incessant hurrying to have
dinner ready on time, hanging
up the phone mid-sentence
when he pulls to the curb. She's
discovered wine and valium
leaves her numb by the time
he stumbles in from the corner bar,
avoiding swollen slobber lips, railing.
If he climbs on she doesn't hear him
ask, did you come?

Mom

Shimmering glass birds vibrate,
taking flight on the end
of rusty metal spikes,
Mom's favorite knickknack.
In their bedroom closet hangs a coat,
a pair of flats on the floor.
After she died he never slept
in the bedroom again,
instead the living room couch
where he called out
her name. I slept in her bed
the night she died,
spirits came,
two matching
lamps took sudden flight,
detached camera flashes exploded,
Sundance whistles blowing; dancers
        on the plastic rug protector by the door.
We couldn't bring ourselves
        to box those remaining items,
too final to close the lid,
        to stop the flight.

Road Rage

On the way to the university,
I hit every light red, plus
two trains, one stalled.
Idiots run red lights,
tear through stop signs,
causing adrenaline rushes.
Red River flooding,
again,
my four-mile trail
to work is now a snaking
network of clay dikes and detours.
I pound my forehead with my fist,
pull my hair,
scream, jerk the steering
wheel, snap my head back and forth.

I remember my brother,
freshly back from Viet Nam,
sitting in the left turning lane,
an angry Marine glare
perpetually on his face,
staring down a driver turning
left from the opposite corner.
He locked eyes with the driver,
who slammed to a stop,
a bloody fight ensued.

I'm careful
not to make eye contact,
plead for patience
with the cars,
trains, the river,
and whoever drives them.

My Grandmother Was Strong

My grandmother was strong enough
to break buffalo ribs with bare hands,
tanned hides, dug turnips, cool and deep
within the earth, moved across the prairie
in smoked hide moccasins, smelled
of wild onions and peppermint, gathered
berries and medicines, wove Wesakechak
stories during snowy winter nights, the bark
of coyote nearby, showered by northern lights,
as she danced with ancestor spirits.

Voyageurs "Lard Eaters"

Home from school hungry, I grab
two slices of Wonder Bread,
best thing since sliced bread,
reach in the fridge for the one pound
square box of lard wrapped in crisp white paper,
cut a thick wedge, lay it on the bread,
shower a generous layer of sugar,
and top with the second slice.
The voyageur Thompson tells of his meal
of bannock bread and lard.
What would he think of my lard brick
that no longer needs rendering, of Slo Baked,
sliced, prepackaged, soft, revolutionary
new way of baking bread that eliminated
holes in slices, reduced calories,
reduced incidents of beriberi and pellagra.
The quiet miracle—although the wheat
has been stripped of its natural nutrients through bleaching.
Howdy Doody and Buffalo Bob Smith telling him
Wonder Bread builds strong bodies 8 ways!
Look for the package with brightly colored balloons.
The colored bag ties tell you which day of the week
the loaf was baked,
Blue Monday
Green Tuesday
Orange Wednesday
Red Thursday
White Friday
Yellow Saturday
Sunday was a day of rest,
day of quiet miracles.

Muskrat Tails

1. Muskrat Tails

Skin the muskrats,
nail the skins to a board
and put up high
so dogs don't get 'em,
boil the muskrats over a slow fire
using just enough water to cover the meat,
when almost cooked, add Red River
potatoes, prairie onions,
wild turnips. Pour everything
in a cast iron kettle, bury the kettle
in the hot ashes. Take the muskrat tails
and stick them in the hot ashes,
after only a few minutes
peel the skin off.
This treat, delicate and white
as snow, is best eaten immediately,
served as Indian hors d'oeuvres.

2. LeGren

After the first freeze
go out into the Turtle Mountain
bush to your favorite spot
you keep secret from all your cousins
and pick some chokecherries
when they are sweetest,
and you won't have to fight
mosquitoes or ticks.
Have your grandkids help you pick.
Pound the chokecherries
on your kookum's
flat rock using her oval-shaped
pounding rock that fits snug in your hand,

grind the pits as finely as you can,
shape the pounded berries into small
cookies, and place under an old window screen,
put on top the lean-to shed where they will dry
slowly in the North Dakota sun.
Store in a cracker tin.
On Thanksgiving Day put a couple cookies-
worth in a cast iron skillet
with some water and set over a low fire,
when soft and starting to smell like summer,
add sugar and a pinch of flour to thicken,
stir in some bacon grease and fry it up a little,
put a small amount on all your relatives' plate,
kids too, and tell them they have to eat it, pits and all.

3. Bangs (Fry Bread)

Put about four cups of flour in a glass bowl.
Add six to nine teaspoons of baking powder.
Toss in a dash of sugar.
Mix well with fork.
Make a "well" in the center of the flour.
Now here comes the secret:
use canned milk, the commodity kind
works fine. Open with one of those
church key can openers. While you're doing
this be running your tap water hot,
as hot as it gets.
In a one cup measuring
cup, pour a half cup of milk; now fill it up
with the hot water, so you have half cup
mixed with hot water.
Pour into the well of flour. Use a total
of two and one-half cups. Quickly mix
together, but don't stir too much!
Dough should be sticky. Sprinkle flour

on dough and knead it around lightly
until it's not so sticky. Cover with a white
embroidered dish cloth your mom
made while in boarding school
and let the dough rest. Flatten the dough
with your hands or a rolling pin.
Not too flat. Cut into any shape
you like. You can cut into rectangles,
then cut a slit in the middle and fold
one of the ends through it to make
a nice little twist like Kookum showed me.
In a cast iron skillet melt some lard
about two inches deep. You know the grease
is just right when you drop a round
piece of dough in and it sinks
to the bottom then pops right back up.
Turn your bread the second it pops back up.
You can eat this one right away
to make sure it's cooked all the way through.
Watch carefully for dough to turn a golden brown,
turn it over and fry on other side. Use a long fork
to take out of the pan and put on a cookie sheet
with paper towels to absorb the grease,
be careful, these will float to the ceiling!
You can put butter on them, drizzle with honey,
roll in sugar, dunk in Juneberry pudding
or wild rice soup, and tell the kids
they will have to wait until dinner.

Vacant

Windows watch me
drive by, filmy eyes,
gauzy lace curtains
tear and billow in the wind
waving to passersby
in gentle despair
no roads lead to it
only well-tended fields
of soybeans,
a yarny blanket.
The house sleeps quietly
unraveling its history
through broken glass dreams.

Slow Time

She rises to stoke the old Monarch stove,
her place in the bush more a cabin than a house,
puts a pan of water on so I can wash my face,
get dressed then head out to school
where I'll teach fourth-graders reading and times
tables. She puts on her calico dress and well-worn

apron sewn from torn clothes others have worn.
She will busy herself about the stove
getting ready for lunch time.
She still chops wood, stacks it by the house,
and waits my return from school,
combs her hair, puts rouge on her face,

pins her curls and she's ready to face
the day, same as before, rutted and worn
as the reservation road I take to school.
She sits on her couch, away from the stove,
listens to the quiet of her house,
shuffles cards and thinks about old times.

The wringer washer needs filling, hard time
carrying water from nearby slough, facing
an uphill climb winding back to the house
through trees, leaves ticking, the path well worn.
To boil water she puts more wood in the stove.
The cool steam greets me when I return from school.

I help hang clothes on the line as the school
bus rattles by, kids waving. When it's suppertime
she brings in a load of wood and feeds the stove,
makes rubbaboo and fry bread. I feed my face
while she puts her tea kettle on the stove. Worn
out from work inside and outside the house,

and thinking of days gone by, she houses
many memories, wishes she had gone to school
past the third grade. Sitting in the worn
corner of her couch, she calls evenings "slow time,"
shuffles her cards that no longer have faces,
while boiling drops dance like tears on the hot black stove.

Night time we listen to the snaps in the stove.
As the house cools she schools
her cards, faces absent, shuffling, shuffling, worn.

At Boarding School

At boarding school, Mom learned to knit.
I'd hold a skein of yarn in my arms.
sway back and forth while she
wrapped it into a ball.

At boarding school, Mom learned to embroider.
Kitchen towels held names,
one for each day of the week I used
when washing and drying dishes each night.

At boarding school, Mom learned to darn socks.
On quiet winter nights sitting by a lamp
head bowed over a light bulb with my white
cotton sock stretched over it, carefully
weaving frayed edges together.

At boarding school mom learned to wash clothes.
Worked in the school's laundry, bluing the whites,
ran clothes through the mangle, careful
not to catch an arm, hang on clothes lines.

At boarding school, Mom learned to sew.
Made all my clothes, even when I
complained that kids made fun of me,
my homemade skirts, dresses,
pants and darned socks, saying we were poor.

She sewed aprons, over-the-head bibs,
wrap around waist every day calico ones,
gauzy frou-frou ones for holidays,
starched stiff, with sheer pockets,
fancy hanky tucked in,
wide ribbons to make a bow.

At boarding school Mom learned to clean.
Detailed to bathroom toilets with a toothbrush,
washed walls, scrubbed floors on hands and knees,
scraped dirt from corners with a butter knife,

At boarding school, Mom learned to cook.
And every day at home donned an apron,
and baked and cooked
and baked and cooked.
On holidays she wore the fancy
sheer frou frou apron with wide
starched ribbons, hanky tucked
in pocket, embroidered
with exquisite lace,
hands aching stiff from arthritis
had me tie a pretty bow.

At boarding school girls
were taught to be domestic servants,
trained to be housewives
they didn't have a choice,
nuns stood stern, with rulers in hand,
my mother mastered the art
of housekeeping.

Mom taught me how to knit,
and darn,
and embroider,
and wash and hang clothes
sew aprons, iron, wash walls,
scrub floors, scrape corners.
Exhausted, I refused to learn
to cook. The ghost of Pratt
whispered in her ear,
and she told me I would
never find a husband.

Regret

I am blind to the morning star,
I hide from the sweet rain,
trample the fragile orchid.
Tears bead my face,
I wear regrets around my neck
laced tight.
I exist only to gather storms,
but why when I could see the storm
coming black from the west
did I not cut all the full peony blooms
and bring them safely inside?
Now, heavy heads lie
splintered and piled wet,
clinging to the cold cement,
wearing hail as a beaded necklace.

A Box Labeled String Too Short to Use

for Carol Davis

In winter we butchered a pig, placed in a tub
and stored on top the cabin; we rendered fat
from pork; pounded cream to butter, lowered
in the well, cooling with the eggs;

caught gophers and roasted them on a stick, eaten
with raw or roasted navoos. Venison sliced
in strips we hung by the stove to dry, then stored
in calico bags with peppermint to keep

the ants at bay. Uncles hunted rabbits,
skinned and boiled to make a rubbaboo.
Grandpa trapped muskrats in spring, boiled
them up added potatoes and wild onions,

turnips, or esquibois, poured in cast
iron kettle and put in the oven.
For a special treat we roasted muskrat tails
on top the old wood stove or stuck in camp

fire embers, stripped the skin, enjoyed.
We ate the older hens for Sunday supper,
killed a skunk before he sprayed, then took
his oil, bottled and stored it in a medicine

room, used it for pneumonia and flu;
went with Kookum early mornings before
the spirits woke to gather plants and roots
for medicine, hung them upside down

on cabin beams. We gathered wild hops
on banks of creeks to use as yeast in dough,
pulled sweet cattails from the slough,
aunties danced to loosen the mud around

the roots we used as leavening for bread.
Stored half the vegetables from the garden
in a cellar under the floor, the other half
fit into a six-foot pit outside, then set

a door over the vegetables, hay
on top the board and sealed with rich black dirt.
Uncle Joe traveled to Elbow Woods
to trade oak posts and berries for Hidatsa

sisters—corn, beans, pumpkins, and squash—
canned the rest to have a taste of summer
when forty below; Kookum pounded chokecherries
on rocks, shaped them into cookies and dried

on top of the roof, a screen to fool the crows,
reconstituted the cookies at Christmas with water,
bacon grease, sugar, and a bit of flour,
fried in cast iron skillet on the stove.

For breakfast we ate leftovers from supper,
ate anything not considered a rodent
or crawling on the ground. In summer we carried
the old wood stove outside, placed it under

the cool shade of aspen tree boughs.
Mother made syrup from brown sugar and coffee,
bacon grease we used in oatmeal and anything
else we wanted to pour it over, including

our hair, which made it shine like a beaver's pelt.
We had running water, ran down the hill
to the slough and fetched it, hauled it back
to wash our clothes, even in the winter

hung outside, frozen stiff and flat.
On winter nights a three boiled tea we made
by melting snow in a corn syrup pail, skimming
rabbit "beads" that floated to the top,

when water boiled threw in a handful of leaves,
removed it from the fire, then boiled again,
three times it boiled, we drank without sugar,
because we usually didn't have any by then.

Stormy winter evenings we sat around
the stove eating pukkons, picked in the fall,
and stored on top of the lean-to roof. We listened
to stories of tawn kiyash, buffalo hunts,

battles with Nadowessi, and Kookum
passed her sarsaparilla all around,
she stashed her money in Bag Balm cans, buried
them somewhere in the bush under a birch tree,
made quilts from Grandpa's Bull Durham tobacco
bags with army blanket batting. Stored
in blue glass jars with lids her buttons and ribbons,
made dresses sewn from floral flour sacks

and sequined moccasins from army canvas,
Aunt Mary braided old brown socks into rugs,
cut Ojibwe floral designs from wool
material, embroidered onto rugs.

Mops they cut from old dress shirts and rags,
curled our hair with rags or wrapped brown paper
around tin strips cut from Prince Albert tobacco cans,
rolled up our hair and crimped the curls in.

Plastic curtains worked just fine, susurrus
in the summer breeze. Sheer curtains from
the bundles used as netting over cribs.
The heart of a stump so old the center had turned

to a powder so fine we could use it as talcum.
Newspapers and gift wrappings made festive wallpaper,
put tissues that wrapped apples and oranges
in bloomer drawers as potpourri, the lovely

scented tissue from peaches straight to the outhouse.
Dad kept crooked nails hammered them straight;
he flattened tin cans to shingle the chicken coop.
I wore the same dress to school for a week,

shared clothes with sisters and cousins. Not to waste
water, we took a bath on Sunday nights,
tried not to be the last one in the tub.
When out of kerosene Ma put sugar

in a rag, twisted it tight, soaked
in grease and lit, or cut the tab from baby's
shirt, the part that pinned it to the diaper, broke
out the inside of a button, and slid

the tab on through, then placed the button on
the side of a bowl of grease, used this little
lamp until we could afford kerosene.
Last, hugs were saved for those we love.

Identity

The Day Before I Stopped Speaking

The day before I stopped speaking,
Sister Genevieve caught me writing

in my Big Chief notebook
I hate this school

repeatedly in perfect Palmer,
each page topped with the requisite

J.M.J., Jesus, Mary, and Joseph.
exquisite J's, swirly M,

filling line after line.
Sent to Mother Superior's office

I sat small as she flipped through
the pages, red-faced against her white

wimple, she stormed down the long hall
opening all the classroom doors,

ordered me across her lap, lifted
my homemade wool flannel jumper

baring my Goodwill bloomers,
smacked the wooden paddle

until my cries filled the open
classrooms like lines in a notebook.

Identity Crisis

In fourth grade the nun wanted to know what nationality
I was. I asked Mom. *Tell her you are Indian*
from the Turtle Mountains. I told the nun. She smiled,
hard, sucking in air. Oh, you are Indian from India, yes!
She brought me brass elephants, incense holders, and books
to write a report for the class. I can still see the B+.
The kids believed me, called me squaw, jerked my braids,
woo woo, stinking savage injun! She has germs, tag!
Now you have her germs! In middle school I was Chinese,
In high school Polynesian, although I told the history teacher
my father was Indian and attended the very boarding school
she mentioned. *So your father was a chief!* All eyes shot
towards me, I slowly nodded yes.

The Portland Indian Center waved me in and I was taken
in by the American Indian Movement, Indian Power,
fist pumps, marches, and demonstrations. Tied an eagle
feather in my hair, wore beaded fringe that ticked and swayed,
bone chokers, soft-soled moccasins, glared at white folks
who dared to stare.

One day I heard the drum at Delta Park, saw the Butterfly
Dance, calico dresses, winged arms spread wide, feet
lightly touching the earth. I saw the Owl Dance
and the War Dance, white buckskin-dressed men, regal.
Time stood still as I watched the dancers, moccasin feet
patting the earth. I couldn't breathe for the beauty.
In the shadows of the tipis I tried to capture the steps.
The drum stopped, I overstepped.

How do they know when to stop?

My first dance outfit was a butter-yellow wool flannel shawl,
soft buckskin dress found in a reservation trading post,
pink shell earrings, braids wrapped in fur, west coast style,
Apache moccasins copied from a Geronimo poster.

Elders told me, *listen to the drum,*
it is your heartbeat,
the drum will tell you when to stop.

I listened to the drum's heartbeat
and danced.

I danced the Rabbit dance
at Turtle Mountain,
Crow Hop at Ft. Yates,
danced to achingly beautiful
49er hand drum songs that brought
out the northern lights over
New Town one warm August night,
joined Fancy Shawl dancers at Ft. Totten.

Then the Jingle Dress dancers
of Red Lake gifted me a Medicine
dress, Ziibaaska'iganagooday,
and elders counseled me,

You are Anishinaabe Ikwe,
this is a healing dress, dance
zigzag to chase away all that's
not good, don't dance backwards
or your life will be backwards,
tangle your jingles and your life
will be tangled, spin in circles
and your life will spin in circles.

I listened to the drum,
I danced zig zag,
I couldn't breathe for the beauty.
I danced,
I danced,
I stopped on time.

Brass Candlesticks

The candy man knelt in front
of the candy machines,
two headed, held
up by a brass pedestal,
twenty-five cents for peanuts or Reese's Pieces.
Bag on the floor he
gently twists the tops
sweeps the coins into his bag,
fills the canisters to half full
takes out a rag, shines the brass,
carefully folds it. Backing out
the door, he bows low
making sure no peanuts are left behind.

Why do I think of my sins?
Kneeling in penance,
hands folded in prayer,
twenty-five cents lights candles
perched on brass candlesticks,
seeking favors from saints,
a silent vigil, power of goodness
over darkness of evil.
Bless me father . . .
genuflecting from the pew,
bowing low,
I leave my sins behind.

Respite

Hurtling through mountain passes
the semis blasted
all adrenaline out of me
I pause at continent's divide.

Father Belcourt

Father George Anthony Belcourt
has the unique distinction of having
amassed a fortune during his ministry.
After his retirement he founded
and built the Farmers Bank of Rustico.
It was built of island sandstone
according to his own design, and stands
as an imposing monument to his fame.

Sell all that you own and distribute the money
to the poor, and you will have treasure in heaven. Luke 18:22.

Warrior

for Ed Edmo

Remember when we marched
for fishing rights in Washington,
eating salmon at Frank's
Landing? Alcatraz,
Camp Adair, anti-war marches,
taking over the BIA, Civil Rights
racism sessions, the pain
and hurt? Wounded Knee '73 has faded
from lips but the fire still burns
in our hearts.
My friend, you have seen the world
through wine-colored bottles
of Tokay and Thunderbird;
in a drugged state of euphoria
you became a tall powerful warrior.
No, I won't call you a sellout
if you live in an apartment with a sauna,
a swimming pool, and marry a white woman,
because you paid your dues, my friend,
you paid your dues. You are a warrior.

Tribal ID Card

1.

I'm a card-carrying Indian, me,
One-half blood quantum, mixed blood,
half-breed, Metis, Michif, Bois Brule,
Burnt Thigh, Pembina Chippewa,
Anishinaabe, Ojibwe, Salteaux, French,
Bungi, and Cree, a drop of Assiniboine,
a tish of Irish. I nearly became a full
blood once during a tribal blood quantum
family dispute, but the case was thrown out.
My tribal ID photo, taken at Turtle
Mountain Band of Chippewa Bureau of Indian
Affairs enrollment office, shows a plump, shiny,
brown face and coal black hair. My great-grandmothers
are Woman Facing the Sun and Has Respect
for the People. My grandfathers were voyageurs,
fur trappers, Catholic, wearers of ceinture fléchée
woven during dark frozen nights in forts
along the Red River of the North.

2.

St. Ann was patron saint of the voyageurs.
In the name of the Father, Son, and Holy Ghost,
protect our rum this high wine we bring to trade
with the savages, one quart for a hundred pounds
of manoomin, one quart for thirty buffalo hides,
two quarts for five bear skins and twenty beaver pelts,
to dress the wealthy in London.

3.

Louis Riel's mother was a Lajimodiere.
He was Metis, hanged for treason
against the Canadian government,
led two rebellions, fought for Indian land,
born one-eighth Indian,
not enough blood to be an enrolled,
not enough for a tribal ID card.

Le Nicknames

If you live on my rez
you inevitably have a nickname,
often forever to your chagrin
something you said or did
sometimes a mix of French or Cree,

Wimp, Soody, Two Ton, K O, Fuzzie,
Bunzie, Mickey, Porky, Mort, Penny,
Chid, Chid-a-Boo, Big Head, Slim,
Tup Tup, Joe Fa, Joe La She Gah, Nat,
Farmer, Small, Genelee, Too Led, Old Bill,
Young Bill, Bishee Led, Choolium, Postum,
Jesus Christ, Boots, Booky, Big Kid, Tonto,
Diddy Foo, Fatty, Frog, Socks, Bird, Baby Socks,
La Vah Zess, Squank, Maggie, Moosy, MeChif
Piiked, Che Joe, Bow Legged, Papino, Mokey,
Chakes, Skinny Cat, Shy, The Rev, Girlee, Sonny,
Buddy, Lou Lou, Gus Cheesy, Boogy Red, Le Dog,
Skullo, Che-yum, Che John, Kiss-ond, Doo Dush,
Che Chit, Tee Tish, Bimbo, Jumbo, Doc, Tiny,
Chick, LaJip, Chicken, Pony, Joe Louis, Suub
Grizz, Sir, La Pyas, Gum Ass, Pa Tack, Joe La Pinnaise,
Chunks, Stuffy, Red, Mush, Donuts, City, Sheep Man
Tomato, Johnny Cake, Chee Chee, Gii Gii, Buth,
Cee Cee, FeFe, Yoyo, Jojo, Joe, Curley, Billy Bum, KK, Baby,
Son Son, La Bitch. Le Nish, Cutty, So Sweet, Chugger,
Junior, Billy Biyou, Pop Corn, Joe Fuzz, Scabby Joe
Ma Karoo, Beezard, Dummy, Dubby, Tum Tum,
Tweet Tweet, Pay-i-shish, Joe Beef, Joe Bullfrog,
Beef, Sissy Girl, Baby Girl, La Truck, Tuk It A Tux,
Le Job, Le Zhun, Rabbit, Le Groo, Uncle Groovy
Grandpa Groovy, Sister, Tiny, Big D, Buttchis,
Che Boy, Che Girl, La Bullette, La Gaulette, String Bean,
Buffalo, Blue Eyes, Boston, Foo Fee, Bolix, Popsy,

Chip Chee, Zhull, Wahbee, Pugsy, Mugs, Tic Tic,
Bah Bish, La See Do, Che Bun, Tahnish, Nahnish,
Swede, Chook, Chip, Twiggy, Tippy, Badger, Asshole,
Kumish, Koosish, Chi Gaw, Chi Garso, Didifoo,
Chi Boy, Chi Fe, Chickadee, Pusch, Bah, Cheesh,
Chi Girl, Le Grah Souris, LaGrews, La Kataen, LaChai,
Le Job, Tet Ti Kwasho, LaQuette, La Vyae, La Vieur,
KooKoosh, Chooch, Sky, Pootee, LaShoosh, La Poonk,
Big Head, Bubbins, Puckkon, La Ha Rouge, La Jang, Bugs,
Jingles, Katush, Foxy Pickie, Sneaky Snake, Fatty, Tiny,
Romero, Bucky, Hoover, Bunny, Pinky, Pickles, Skin, Carty,
Snackwell, Kawlige, Quita Minny, Minnie Mouse, Minijigs,
Lushy, Chicket, Whiskey, Shemp, Squints, Gump, Bologna,
Flobee, Dirty Paul, Meat, Grumpy, Potts, Wig, Musky, Chewy,
Spudy, Fuzz, Killer, Bubush, Yoder, DeeDolls, Egg Juice.

I don't have a nickname, wish I did.

Morning Star

In the Yuwipi the spirits
said pray with sweet grass, your prayers
will be carried to the Creator,
we will help you, Woman from the North.

In the inipi the spirits spoke,
you must find your
own way Anishinaabe,
Woman from the North,
for you are not Lakota.
In my dream Grandma Great Walker
said, *find morning star.*

I began a journey.
The Lakota
said, *morning star*
offers wisdom, we get up early each day
to greet the morning star.

The Crow
said, *morning star*
is Red Bear's patron spirit,
giving him untold powers.

Blackfeet said, *morning star*
brought the sweat lodge
to us, the healing lodge.

I traveled to Red Lake,
and asked the Anishinaabe
medicine woman in ceremony,
offering asemaa, tobacco,
tell me about the morning star.

Ho! she said, eyes laughing,
Boozhoo Wabanung Ikwe!
Woman of the North,
it is you, you are Morning Star.

His Feathers Were Chains

Let Him Win

Custer the dandy, dressed
in blue-gray flannel shirt,
knobby buckskin trousers
tucked inside spit-shined

high jackboots, pranced
into Fort Totten on his horse
Vic. Came to inspect his 7th Cavalry
assigned to protect the U.S. boundary.

Fort Totten, located in desolate Dakota
territory, a crumbling hell hole, blazing
summers, blasting bitter cold
winters. Drunken soldiers and high

ranking officers thrown in jail below
the barracks, facing court for failure
to perform military duties, sobered
up and stood at attention as the band

played "Garry Owen." It was Custer's luck
to win at poker, Captain warned his men
to let him win, but a young lieutenant
played his cards and won. Custer sent

orders for him to stay when the 7th Cavalry
reported to Fort Lincoln in preparation for
fighting the Sioux on the Little Big Horn.
A month later the soldier stood at dark attention

as Comanche, a paint horse, survivor
of the showdown, walked into the Fort to be
retired from battle, the chase over, last
bugle call, gate closed.

Ponemah

for Sam

At Ponemah the spiritual
leaders called all the Bear
Clan to come and dance.
Your aunties came to get you.
A sacred staff had fallen
in the middle of the circle,
pipes were brought out
and the smoke of tobacco
plumed high joining makwawag
gathered in the clouds, eagle
bone whistles blew, the warriors
danced in the rain by the lake
singing Anishinabe prayers
too sacred for English.

Shape Shifters

The cavalry calculated one way to destroy
a tribe was to jail the medicine men,
the healers, visionaries, gentle leaders.

An elder told me that's what the 7th Cavalry did at Fort Totten,
anyone caught conducting a ceremony was incarcerated;
the Cavalry threw our medicine men in the fort's cellar jail.

But they showed up that night
and held a ceremony in the village.
The lieutenant, hearing of this, stormed
down to the cellar, unlocked and heaved
open the thick metal door to the room
with no windows, and there they were.

Whitestone Hill

At Whitestone "battlefield"
a granite monument of a bugle
boy sounding rally is surrounded
by headstones of fallen Cavalry
soldiers. An American flag snaps
in the wind like bullets through canvas.
On September 3, 1863,
General Alfred Sully's troops
attacked a peaceful tipi camp of Yanktonai,
Dakota, Hunkpapa, and Sihasapa
Lakota, part of a military mission
to punish participants of the Dakota
Conflict of 1862. The 6th Iowa Cavalry
detachment had discovered a camp
of four hundred lodges, young men away
from camp hunting buffalo. Sully
ordered the bugler to sound rally,
and with chevrons blazing the attack
began. In panic and desperation, fleeing
mothers tied their babies onto dog
travois and screamed them out of camp
as Sully ordered

Shoot anything in a blanket!
Shoot dogs, horses. Shoot holes in kettles!

Berries had been pounded
and dried, medicines hung
from tipi poles, five hundred
thousand pounds of buffalo
meat had been prepared
against the long bitter winter
ahead. Following the massacre
troops heaped bodies on

the tons of buffalo and burned
the pile, the melted tallow running
in streams down the hilly terrain.

As I sat in a nearby concrete
cairn of field stones, a meadowlark
landed on top the bugle boy's head,
his song piercing the fluted silence,
his chevron blazing.

Manifest Destiny

Because of your cartography
and Sakakawea, your slave,
you painted mountain
valleys and river routes
in your journal, and opened
the flood gates of extinction
to our coastal relatives,
the Anishinaabe peacefully traded
for shells with buffalo hides and root medicines.
Garrison dammed the peaceful Missouri
and flooded the Mandan Hidatsa river villages.
Your journals written in fancy calligraphy
further practiced in painstaking form through
the plains and mountain routes,
yet your orthography was atrocious
while Manifest Destiny just rolled along.
The route was mapped out,
the long prophesized flow of chimookomon
came rolling through, doling
out smallpox blankets to the Mandan.
Paint that in your cartography,
make that look pretty with your calligraphy.
Do you have a correct
and acceptable spelling of genocide
in your orthography?

Smallpox

I follow my kookum
through dense underbrush
to gather red willow bark.
She stops, motions to three
mounds, piles of rocks mossed over
and says *smallpox!*
She admonishes me not
to pick anything fearing
disturbing the mounds
will unleash the dreaded disease.

The state health workers set
up a booth at our pow wow
handing out diabetes information,
also giving away army blankets,
green, itchy. Walking by, Kookum fell
back from the booth and hurried away.

Eeee! Do they have smallpox?

Prairie Drive

Hawk perched on hay bale,
patient, watching for field mice.
Traffic careens by.

The See Far Place

In all places either remarkable by their position, or by the gearings of the savages, they shall take care to plant high crosses, as it were to take possession of those places in the name of the Catholic religion.
Msgr. J. O. Plessis, instructions given to missionary priests.

On the highest butte
in the Turtle Mountains
a tall cross has been planted.
The Ojibwe call the butte
Atacaamaabiwin, the place
from which to see far. Scouts watched
over plains to the south
flat as a stretched and staked
buffalo hide, waiting for Nadowessi
and when spotted sounded
an alarm by lighting a fire
signaling others deep in the hills,
brush-and-tree-covered
backs of turtle's carapace.

Butte St Paul
named by Reverend George A. Belcourt,
January 25, 1850
when he was caught in a blizzard
and hunkered down by the butte.

The steep, rocky path
lined with swollen chokecherries,
winds its way to the top.
Aroma of sage and sweet grass waft
from freshly cut fields below.

A tall stone and cement cairn emerge,
a defiant red cloth covers the high cross,
Sun Dance sage crowns tied to four corners,
eagle plumes dance in the rising heat
as many-eyed dragonflies keep watch, vigilant.

Battle at Dog Den Butte

Falcon ordered us to gather the carts
in a tight circle that hot summer day.
Our Red River carts two hundred strong
locked tongues, an impenetrable barrier.
Inside the circle oxen, ponies, and buffalo
runners were corralled. I helped the men dig
trenches, then lay with my abinoojiwag.
Thirty of our warriors headed.this way
pursued by Nadowessi, Dakota! Hundreds
strong in full battle dress. Most of our men
enter the safety of our circle. Jerome and Malaterre
are captured! Aicawpow is injured, Ducet's horse
shot. In a barrage of gunfire, the enemy's leader,
White Horse, is killed by Falcon, *He was so beautiful,*
that my heart revolted at the necessity of killing him.
The charge of the Dakota came to an abrupt halt;
they fled from our bullets. The next day,
heading to the Turtle Mountains, a scout
signaled enemy sighted! A circle formed quickly.
Snakes swirled around us, slipping to the side
of their ponies, couldn't aim their guns and arrows
under fat summer bellies. Circling around us
they were easy targets, and soon gave up the battle,
hurtling one last volley of bullets and arrows.
As the Dakota signaled to us they would not
continue the battle, and waved their weapons
in the air, I jumped on top of a cart, my sisters joined me,
stripping from our buckskin dresses
we stood naked before the enemy,

Look we are just women,
come back and fight!
I, the wife of Falcon!

Did You Hear the Boulders Rolling?

for Christine, Maui, HI

Did you hear the boulders rolling last night?
The high mountain storm caused flooding rains
and brought the gentle stream to new heights.

The storm came crashing in right after twilight,
the thunder and roar sounding like a train,
but did you hear the boulders rolling last night?

Trees were torn into the water's violent right
to rage ragged over volcanic rocks again

and bring the gentle stream to new heights.

The storm blew in and mourning doves took flight,
dragonflies abandoned rocks where they had lain.
Did you hear the boulders rolling last night?

Thunder exploded between flashes of light
causing heavy clouds to burst and drain

which brought the gentle stream to new heights.

Pale hibiscus flowers in morning's bright
light, the valley silent from the storm's refrain,

but did you hear the boulders rolling last night?
The storm brought a gentle stream to new heights.

Haleakala

for Daryl

We arrive at Ma'alea harbor
before sunrise. The crew bustling
about preparing the boat for snorkelers.

Haleakala, House of the Sun,
rises 10,000 feet above us.

E ala e Ka la i kahikina
I ka moana
Ka moana hohonu
Pi'i ka lewa
Ka lewa nu'u
I kahikina
Aia ka la.
E ala e!

Awaken! Arise!
The sun in the east
From the ocean
The ocean deep
Climbing to the heaven
The heaven highest
In the east
There is the sun
Awaken!

I stand port side facing Haleakala,
rising radiance fills the House
of the Sun, overflows,
shimmering like lava gold,
flowing to the ocean,
sweeping me to the heavens,
awake.

His Feathers Were Chains

At a small town in South Dakota
I stopped to rest and saw an Indian
on a horse welded together using
farm implements and planted
on the lawn next to the Sioux Motel.

His war bonnet was a sickle bar,
his shield a disc blade,
his feathers were chains,
a splicer connector formed
his mouth into a permanent
oval, his horse's body was a barrel,

a harrow for a tail, his hoofs support
brackets. I found him there and heard
a war cry from his mouth like howls
in my chest. Is one a warrior only
when reveille is heard? Forgive me

friends, but he was there
at Wounded Knee, Little Big Horn,
Washita, Sand Creek, Whitestone Hill,
and has a harrowing tale
to tell, staked to this earth,
his feathers were chains,
his blood a rusty red.

Thin White Heat

Chippewa Winter

The trees
have long since combed their hair.

and stand sentinel
watching for spring's ensign embrace

arms patient
fingers paint the pale sky.

A drumbeat drifts
across the silent plain, the wind

carries a song
through bitter blue air,

clear and free
of pain, perhaps a warrior's death

song thawed from an earlier time.

Buffalo Call

My great-grandfather
and wife left their winter
village along the Red River
to hunt for buffalo
that starvation winter.

Buffalo calling was a gift
he received through vision.
Carrying his buffalo stone
bundle they traveled
through silent omnivorous
snow to old hunting grounds.

He calls and a buffalo
appears over the hill,
shoots and is knocked
off his horse, too weak
to get up. She makes a fire,
feeds him wiiaas.

Others from the village
came looking for them,
following the smoke.
The villagers dance
and feast on the gift
of buffalo meat,
singing thanks to the spirit
of the great prairie bull.

Dakota January

The moon of bone-cracking cold
of Styrofoam crunch snow,
the snow-blind moon
the moon of white-outs,
short days, long nights,
the moon of blizzards,
of popping tree limbs,
the moon of thirty days below zero,
of windchill advisories,
frostbit, blackened skin,
the moon of frozen lakes,
the least heat moon,
the moon of white suns,
communion discs,
the Alberta clippers moon.
Giiwedin, blasts from the north,
howling a frigid refrain.
Diamond dust ice-crystal dogs cup
the sun's brilliant face
resting on a pillar,
a second set, a pale mirage
reflected in frozen snow,
polished to a shine.
Snow rivers flow across
the plains, toward
a pale horizon.
Giiwedin roars and I'm surrounded
by a circle of ghost buffalo,
warmed by their breath.

Windigo

The tribal store is packed with Indians stocking
up on milk, white bread, bologna, and Pampers,
a holiday atmosphere as we whip up and down
the aisles. Warnings of a blizzard sound on the tribal
radio station. To the north a black cloud hangs
heavy as a wool blanket. All that night Giiwedin roared.
Morning and the rez is clamped in the frozen jaws
of a northern plains blizzard, nothing moving
through roof-high drifts, the windows frosted Ojibwe
floral designs, more fantastic than any beadwork.
Scraping Prairie roses from my window I see wind-
whipped snow thick as quilt batting. I keep busy
with beadwork, sewing, turning jingles, make hot black
tea with milk, wishing for Kookum's wood stove.
Giiwedin howling at minus thirty, fifty-below wind chill,
snow blowing horizontally. I make bannock with wild
rice soup, worry about the furnace frantically working
to keep the house warm, the radio the only other voice,
thin solace. Cabin fever sets in, and now I'm pacing
the oval patterned braided rug no interest in radio, food.
Giiwedin is relentless. Windigo has raced over from Lake
Nipissing, across Miskwaa-gamiiwi-zaaga'igan to my village
of Sibising, he latches his icy fingers to my roof, I hear nails
screech, beams moan—stomach clenches in terror. Kookum's
warning, *Don't be greedy or Windigo will eat you!* rings in my ears,
and I am frozen, unable to move. Windigo whacks the outside
walls with his icy, bagamaagan, jarring echoes vibrate floorboards
and beams, slowly circling the house, banging walls tearing the roof.
My bedroom wall is hit, shudders horribly, fragile panes rattle,
floor beams expand, each a cannon boom. Huddled, I wait for the house
to explode, shatter in a brittle frozen hiss and I will be consumed.

Log Cabin Dreams

Wrapped tight in a dikinaagan
my parents put my baby brother
in a swing above their bed,
a rope pull, lulled to sleep.
My father stokes the wood stove
while I lie flat under heavy wool quilts
hand sewn squares, a plastic curtain
filler for added warmth. We wake
to a solid block of ice in the wash basin.
Kookum stirs oatmeal,
adds a slug of bacon grease,
braids my hair so tight my scalp tingles.
Mom heats rocks to put in mittens
for the walk to school in twenty-below cold,
sweeps and tamps the clay floor
solid as cement, lays braided
rugs made from bundles
of throwaway cotton dresses.
In Fargo, I turn down the heat,
lie flat under Kookum's quilts
listening to the blizzard outside,
lulled to sleep, tied to dreams
of wood smoke and small round stones.

Forty Below

It's forty below, the angled
southern sun offers a thin

white heat. I pull snow pants
over jeans, Cuddle Duds, long-

sleeved shirt, wool sweater,
Smart Wool socks, fur-lined boots,

down coat, puffy, knitted chook,
wolf fur-trimmed hood, thick

maroon scarf, beaded leather
gloves, rabbit-fur lined.

Lungs catch, then cough
in the frigid air, expelled

in short white puffs
breathed into wool and fur,

smell of animals
sour, damp, dead.

Boots screech on glitter
snow, past flower beds

clenched in sleep under
drifts four feet deep,

crawl in my vehicle
hollow and still,

turn the key, moans,
then a high-pitched scream.

Ultimate Demise

Outlines of leaves are petroglyphs on the white
cement, darling buds blown off by winter winds,
potent reminders of the outline our light
will make in graves when our lives crosswind
cede to time. This voyage we take across
a prairie ocean doesn't have a written script.
We roll with the waves of pain and sometimes lose
too much for our chests to bear, such conflict.
But I will not feel barren on this windswept day,
nor serious about my ultimate demise,
I will hold out for the sweet new buds of May.
As feminine earth sheds her sleep and comes alive,
I'll breathe the serious rain-filled air around me,
demanding my lungs be filled with winds of the sea.

Spring

In a gust of wind
the autumn leaves
skipped across the parking
lot like kids let out
for recess, and something
about their sudden brittle
rush made me think
of the coming winter
and my grief for all
that is dead and dying,
the loneliness of sorrows
strung out on the bitter
wind carrying winter's
frayed blanket. How fragile
this life, how easily crushed
as we pass through
doing the best we can.

I find hope carried
on the wings of returning
wild geese, budding leaves
and melting fields
as I gallop toward spring.

Morning

Summer breeze a softened
sheet of hay, sweet grass, clover,
and younger years, before
the hard heat of the afternoon
seeps into stalagmite bones.
Leaves unfurled, grass
an inviting pool, curtains sigh
into the rest of the day
and I count my blessings
for I am not yet shattered,
not yet silenced, not yet dead.

Dancing with a Whirlwind

Gaabiboonike

Barking geese low overhead startle
me out of my meditation.
It's late August, no tinge of yellow on leaves,
do they hear Gaabiboonike?
Kookum would know what
their early leaving means,
Sitting by the window, shuffling
cards, watching ajidamoo gather nuts,
We'll have an early winter.
Seeing muskrats build their houses high,
It'll be a cold winter.
Last winter I cried in pain, walking
across a campus parking lot,
Giiwedin nodin blowing fifty-six below windchill,
ice crystals stinging needles,
tears and snot frozen on my face,
one eye freezes shut, can't see to open
truck's door, cursing, sitting inside banging
the steering wheel with gloved hands
to get feeling back, my breath pure white
against bitter dark. Now is the time
to prepare for winter, gather bagaanag,
chokecherries, and pembinas,
make thick quilts, pile firewood high.
Like Shingebiss, no matter how many times
I'm kicked, I will keep one red eye open
to the east, trusting in the sun.

Chokecherry Picking in the Turtle Mountains

for Gezik

My grandson wants to pick
chokecherries and make syrup.
We drive through the heart
of the hills to the homestead,

where my grandmother's log
cabin still stands and find
the faint trail, burr oak tree fingers
entwined tightly above, a low

inviting tunnel to the meadow
beyond. Thin clouds stretch lazy
across the sky as if pulled
from cotton batting, yellow

jackets, mosquitoes, no-see-ums,
rustle of snakes. In the quiet
heat, unseen through thick
bushes, my grandson says

I like picking chokecherries
with you Kookum,

and the hills wrap
  a shawl around me,
    woven, entwined.

Gathering Birch Bark

for Jim Northrup

He gave directions to his
maple sugar camp trail
and handed me his favorite knife.
The forest closed in quickly;
trees forming a canopy above.
My granddaughter falls behind,
head bent over her phone.
What the heck you doing?
Tweeting where we're at.
Then a tall birch, a silver pillar,
just off the muddy trail.
An offering of tobacco prayers,
a smooth cut and a layer of bark
unwraps, then instantly scrolls
to its original shape. Turning
to head back, I can't see my
granddaughter. I cry out,
she replies, leaves camouflaging her.
Unnerved by the dense forest, the fading
translucent light, we head back
to the car, taking the wrong fork
and my hairs prickle with panic.
Do you have a compass on that thing?
We double back, reach the road.
Dizzy from adrenaline rush,
I head to the hotel instead of camp.
The next morning I return his blade,
Ho wah, I thought you were lost!
I would have missed my knife!

Crane

for Gezik

We lay on our back rubbing
our hands together to make

the clouds disappear, and they did.
Over by the fountain,

you saw the Sakakawea coin
in the deep well and determined

to fish it out. I sat on the edge
with my newly purchased Ojibwe

language dictionary as you set off
to find a stick by the edge of the coulee.

Your astonishment when part of the dark
bush you reached took flight,

mine as I looked up at the crane
gaining height above the water,

my finger on the word ajijaak,
crane, my doodem.

Birch Bark Biting

I study the spring peeled
bark, gathered when leaves
unfolded.
Thunderbirds, wings spread
wide, gaze back at me.
I peel the amber bark
into thin layers, careful
not to tear claw marks,
place the folded bark in my
mouth, biting down with eye
teeth, closed eyes see designs,
unfold a flower, turtle,
or dragonfly, hold
it to the light, feathery bite
marks glow through
transparent wings.

Anderson Center

Across a field near the river
is an Indian burial mound

where I offer prayers
and talk to the White Pines.

The only mound
in the area spared

from farmers' harrows.
Bones, skulls, beads

sent to universities
and museums

to be researched
for cultural construct

particularities, patrilineal
life cycles, holistic sacred rituals,

ethnocentric displacement
coming from a world view

of western settler colonization.
I heard

a woman singing
an ancestral song

borne from the clearing
above graves, now fields

of researched and modified corn.

Throat Song

He pulled a map
from the plane's
seat pocket and showed
me the island in Nunavut
he was from. He said he
was a throat singer,
would I like to listen to a song?

There are two of us
we face each other
hands on shoulders.

He handed me earphones
soft as pillows,
hooked up his iPhone,
tapped the screen.

This is my favorite.

I closed my eyes
and was transported
to another world.
In the darkness
a kaleidoscope of
god particles danced
on the outer corners
of my eyes,
energy force carriers,
the glue that holds
matter together,
and when the song ended
they fell like soft glitter
to the frozen field below.

Dakota Summer

In the early 1930s
Mom would sleep
on outside cots
when prairie days
were long and sweltering,
She swore the heat would
well from the ground at night.
Grandma would wet sheets,
draping them over her
in a bid to cool her off.

I need cool quiet when I write.
Today the cicadas' incessant high
pitch scream distracting and irritating.
Now the midnight air
a thick blanket.
I head to a field and lie down.
I need Grandma to wrap me in sheets
wet from cool well water.
I need cicadas to stop screaming
how hot the night.
I need to find my muse, lost
in restless prairie dreams.

Waves

Walking the long, curved beach
waves boom then hiss to shore
and swipe away my footprints,

as death will wipe away
even my shadow, no sand cast left.

For now, it seems I can live
forever, the ocean's heave,
my exhaled breath,
rivulets of remnant waves
rippling across my feet.

Sleeping at the Fort Totten Bed and Breakfast

I'll have dreams, I thought,
exhausted from the day spent
sitting in the room where my grandfather
was beaten, the dining room he left hungry,
the dorm where he was made to sit under urine-
damp sheets, the jail under the boys' dorm
where he was sent for speaking Chippewa,
joining others singing their death songs,
the runaways, the cold, the deaths.

I'm offered a variety of rooms in the former
captain's house, all with a decorated theme.
In each, windows facing the prairie
are built high so the soldiers could sit
and fire into oncoming warriors.
The windows facing the parade ground
tall and slender.

I choose the lacy curtained Norwegian
room, uneasy at sleeping in such comfort.
I stash the ticking alarm clock
under a velvet cushion.

I woke to early morning
pre-dawn light, a dreamless sleep noted
with relief. Then, a single beam of light,
a thin ray, pierced the center of a lacy prairie

rose. The spear of light became a kaleidoscope
of sparks, fireworks, rainbows, silent explosions,
faceted wheeling lights dancing. When the atoms
shifted, the earth moved and I upon it, weeping
for the beauty, and for the children.

Exploring the Dungeons at Fort Totten Boarding School

for Oliver Gourd

Red bricks, whitewashed.
Dakota children, Whitewashed.

You refused to speak English,
Trap door raised to the dungeon.

Today, an orange marble found.
Oliver, is this your marble?

I Will Die

after Cesar Vallejo

I will die Saturday
at seven o'clock
during Grand Entry;
on Monday riding a bike
in Italy; I will die
in a Harlem deli.
I will die late evening
when a texting driver
crosses the freeway
median; at 5:00 a.m. in Fargo
a vehicle and train crash.
I will die flung on the prairie during a tornado.
I will die frozen in a North Dakota blizzard.
I will die beaten; my brittle bones broken.

Whirlwind, a Spirit Dancing

I'm six years old running on a narrow
prairie trail barefoot, braids flying, listening
to the whirr and tick of dragonfly wings, loud
in the thick summer heat, when suddenly I'm
engulfed in a rotating wind, my skirt
dancing wildly around my legs.
Whirlwinds, gizhibaayaanimad,
often appearing on sunny days
are believed to have sacred
power by plains tribes. They
are considered to be stirred
up by the rotation of dragonfly
wings. The whirlwind released
its grip and continued down
the trail tall and thin,
before wheeling
out of sight
that day
I danced
with a
whirl
w
i
n
d

Ginew

The insistent wailing of the train.
The low rumbling thunder.

The baby's coffin,
no larger than a flight bag.

The train hushes
into the blue black
V of eternity ahead.
The rails pull up behind,
between them
silence like a blanket.

Glossary

Note from the author: Ojibwemowin was originally a spoken, not written, language. For that reason, spellings will vary depending on the region. I apologize to the reader for any mistakes.

abinoogiwag – grandchildren
ajidamoo – squirrel
ajijaak – crane
Anishinaabe – human being; man, woman, child
asema – tobacco
bagaanag – nuts
bagamaagan – war club
boozhoo – hello
ceinture fléchée – Metis sash
Chimookoman – White man, literally Long Knives
dikinaagan – cradleboard
doodem – clan
Gaabiboonike – Winter Maker
IHS – Indian Health Service
ikwe – woman
Inipi – sweat lodge ceremony
giiwedin or **giiwedin nodin** – north or north wind
Kookum – Grandmother
makwawag – bears
manoomin – wild rice
metis – mixed blood
Miskwaa-gamiiwi-zaaga'iganing – Red Lake
Nadowessi – Sioux, literally Snake in the Grass
Navoos – wild prairie turnips
pembinas – cranberries
rouge – red blush

rubbaboo–rabbit soup

shingebiss–duck

Sibising–Belcourt, North Dakota

tawn kiyash–long time ago

Wabunung–Morning Star

Wesakechak–Sacred being (Cree)

Windigo–a supernatural being that has a desire to kill and eat its victim

wiiaas–white fat

Yuwipi–Lakota healing ceremony

Acknowledgments

Migwech to friends, family, and colleagues who continue to be supportive of my work. I'm grateful to be living in the beautiful Turtle Mountains among Ojibwe and Metis/Michif people who have inspired many of these poems.

Migwech to those who read the manuscript and offered comments. Thank you Heid Erdrich and North Dakota Poet Laureate Larry Woiwode for early readings and suggestions; Jill Kandel for her deeply appreciated and valued suggestions.

I'm thankful to Vermont Studio Center for time and space to write.

Previously published poems:

North Dakota Is Everywhere: An Anthology of Contemporary North Dakota Poems (North Dakota State University Press, 2015): "String Too Short to Use," "His Feathers Were Chains," "Dakota January," "Slow Time."

Original Local (Minnesota Historical Press, 2013): "Muskrat Tails."

Thunderbird (North Dakota State University Press, 2017): "Birch Bark Biting," "Brass Candlesticks," "Call You a Sellout?" "Gathering Birch Bark," "Haleakala."

Yellow Medicine Review: "Dakota January," "Vacant."

From p. 58, "His Feathers Were Chains," the author acknowledges William Stafford's poem, "A Story I Have to Tell You."

About the Author

Denise K. Lajimodiere is an enrolled Citizen of the Turtle Mountain Band of Chippewa, Belcourt, North Dakota. She has been involved in education for forty-four years as an Elementary Teacher, Principal, and Professor, earning her Bachelor's, Master's, and Doctorate degrees from University of North Dakota. Lajimodiere is a retired Associate Professor from the School of Education, Education Leadership program, North Dakota State University, Fargo. She is one of the founders of the National Native American Boarding School Healing Coalition.

In addition to being an author, Lajimodiere is a traditional Jingle Dress dancer and Ojibwe Birch Bark Biting artist. She lives in a cozy cottage by the lake on the Turtle Mountain Indian Reservation.

About the Contemporary Voices of Indigenous Peoples Series

North Dakota State University Press initiated the Contemporary Voices of Indigenous Peoples Series (CVIP) in 2016. The series is co-edited by Drs. Michael Yellow Bird and Suzzanne Kelley. Yellow Bird, a citizen of the Three Affiliated Tribes of the Fort Berthold reservation in North Dakota, identifies as Arikara ("The People") and Hidatsa ("Willows"). He is an author, teacher, and advocate for decolonization, Indigenous social innovation and creativity, and institutional and environmental systems change. Yellow Bird is Dean of the Faculty of Social Work at the University of Manitoba. Kelley is a long-time teacher, historian, and publisher. She is a *summa cum laude* graduate of the University of Texas at Austin, an award-winning teacher and scholar, and—since her hire in 2015—the first woman publisher in the seventy-year history of NDSU Press. In her publishing career, Kelley has shepherded more than one hundred books through production, many of them from emerging authors that have gone on to win state, regional, and national awards.

The vision behind CVIP is to feature the authentic stories, poetry, and scholarly works of Native Americans, First Nations, Maori, Aborigines, Indians, and more to give voice to contemporary Indigenous peoples. Authors are asked to affirm their Indigenous identity and cultural connections. North Dakota State University Press adheres to a solemn commitment to avoid the damaging impact of cultural appropriation.

Published in the series:

Volume 1 *Apple in the Middle*, young adult novel by Dawn Quigley, 2018

Volume 2 *Stringing Rosaries: The History, the Unforgivable, and the Healing of Northern Plains American Indian Boarding School Survivors*, nonfiction by Denise K. Lajimodiere, 2019

Volume 3 *His Feathers Were Chains*, poetry by Denise K. Lajimodiere, 2020

About the Press

North Dakota State University Press (NDSU Press) exists to stimulate and coordinate interdisciplinary regional scholarship. These regions include the Red River Valley, the state of North Dakota, the plains of North America (comprising both the Great Plains of the United States and the prairies of Canada), and comparable regions of other continents. We publish peer reviewed regional scholarship shaped by national and international events and comparative studies.

Neither topic nor discipline limits the scope of NDSU Press publications. We consider manuscripts in any field of learning. We define our scope, however, by a regional focus in accord with the press's mission. Generally, works published by NDSU Press address regional life directly, as the subject of study. Such works contribute to scholarly knowledge of region (that is, discovery of new knowledge) or to public consciousness of region (that is, dissemination of information, or interpretation of regional experience). Where regions abroad are treated, either for comparison or because of ties to those North American regions of primary concern to the press, the linkages are made plain. For nearly three-quarters of a century, NDSU Press has published substantial trade books, but the line of publications is not limited to that genre. We also publish textbooks (at any level), reference books, anthologies, reprints, papers, proceedings, and monographs. The press also considers works of poetry or fiction, provided they are established regional classics or they promise to assume landmark or reference status for the region. We select biographical or autobiographical works carefully for their prospective contribution to regional knowledge and culture. All publications, in whatever genre, are of such quality and substance as to embellish the imprint of NDSU Press.

We changed our imprint to North Dakota State University Press in January 2016. Prior to that, and since 1950, we published as the North Dakota Institute for Regional Studies Press. We continue to operate under the umbrella of the North Dakota Institute for Regional Studies, located at North Dakota State University.